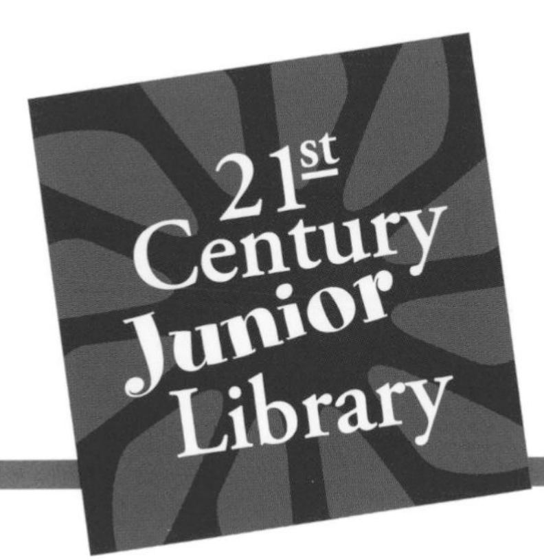

FLOWERS

by Christine Petersen

CHERRY LAKE PUBLISHING * ANN ARBOR, MICHIGAN

Published in the United States of America by Cherry Lake Publishing
Ann Arbor, Michigan
www.cherrylakepublishing.com

Content Adviser: Paul Young, MA, Botany

Reading Consultant: Cecilia Minden-Cupp, PhD, Literacy Specialist and Author

Photo Credits: Page 4, ©iStockphoto.com/alohaspirit; cover and page 6, ©Eric Isselée, used under license from Shutterstock, Inc.; page 8, ©Jessie Eldora Robertson, used under license from Shutterstock, Inc.; page 10, ©Margo Harrison, used under license from Shutterstock, Inc.; cover and page 12, ©Chas, used under license from Shutterstock, Inc.; page 14, ©Tatiana Grozetskaya, used under license from Shutterstock, Inc.; cover and page 16, ©4155878100, used under license from Shutterstock, Inc.; page 18, ©Cornel Achirei, used under license from Shutterstock, Inc.; cover and page 20, ©Chris Curtis, used under license from Shutterstock, Inc.

LIBRARY OF CONGRESS CATALOGING-IN-PUBLICATION DATA
Petersen, Christine.
Flowers / by Christine Petersen.
p. cm.—(21st century junior library)
Includes bibliographical references and index.
ISBN-13: 978-1-60279-275-3
ISBN-10: 1-60279-275-5
1. Flowers—Juvenile literature. I. Title. II. Series.
SB406.5.P48 2008
582.13—dc22 2008008953

Cherry Lake Publishing would like to acknowledge the work of The Partnership for 21st Century Skills. Please visit www.21stcenturyskills.org *for more information.*

CONTENTS

A plant's roots grow down into the soil.

Plant Parts

Each part of your body does a special job. Your lungs breathe. Your eyes see. All the parts work together to help you live and grow.

Plants also have parts that work together. Roots take in water from the soil. Stems bring water to the leaves. The leaves need the water to make food.

Poppies are just one kind of flower.

Plants have flowers, too. They look pretty. Did you know that they also have an important job? Flowers make seeds. Inside each seed is a tiny new plant.

Let's take a closer look at flowers.

Write down the names of your two favorite flowers. Ask five other people to write down their two favorite flowers, too. Guess how many of them put one of your favorite flowers on their lists. Was your guess correct?

Do you see the yellow pollen grains on this flower's stamens?

How Seeds Are Made

Many flowers have colorful **petals**. You must look closely to see the rest of the flower. Between the petals are parts that look like tiny stems. They are called **stamens** and **pistils**.

Stamens make **pollen grains**. A pollen grain is as tiny as a speck of dust. Each stamen is covered with thousands of powdery pollen grains.

Apples are fruits. They grow from the pistils of an apple tree's flowers.

Pollen grains land on top of the pistil and get stuck. The flower is **pollinated**. It can now make seeds.

The pistil changes after the flower is pollinated. It grows into a **fruit**. Fruits protect the developing seeds. Some seeds are smaller than a grain of salt. Others are as large as a football!

Find a flower. Tulips and poppies work well. Ask an adult before you pick one! Gently pull off the petals. Can you see the pistils, stamens, and pollen? Use a magnifying glass if your flower is small.

Hummingbirds are just one kind of animal that visits flowers.

Flower Helpers

Flower petals are like colorful flags. Many petals also smell nice. Animals notice the colors and smells. They come looking for food. Flowers make a sweet juice called **nectar**. Some animals drink the nectar. How can animals help the plants by visiting the flowers?

A butterfly feeds on nectar.

Think of a butterfly walking on top of a milkweed plant. The butterfly's long tongue is like a straw. It sucks nectar from the flowers. The butterfly knocks against the stamens as it walks. Its legs and body get dusted with pollen.

Soon the butterfly flies to a different plant. Pollen falls off of the butterfly. It lands on the new flower's pistil. The flower is now pollinated.

Bees and other insects help pollinate flowers.

There are many animal pollinators. Watch a garden in the summertime. You will see bees and flies on the flowers. Look for beetles, too. Hummingbirds are pollinators. Moths and some bats pollinate flowers at night.

Bats pollinate flowers in deserts and rain forests. They like pale flowers with strong smells. Pretend you are a bat. Why would you choose these flowers? Hint: Bats come out after dark.

Did you say it would be easier to find pale flowers with strong smells in the dark? That is correct!

Wheat is a grass that people grow for food.

Blowing in the Wind

Many flowers are beautiful! But grasses and many trees also have flowers. They can be hard to find. The flowers are small and have no smell. They may not even have petals.

These plants don't use animal pollinators. Wind blows their pollen around. Pollen is carried by wind from one flower to another.

Some flowers grow in deserts.

Maple trees are pollinated by wind. So are wheat and corn.

Keep your eyes open wherever you go. You will find that flowers grow in the most amazing places!

Look for pictures of flowers in old magazines. Cut out some flower pictures. Then look for pictures of bees, butterflies, birds, and other animals that pollinate flowers. Make a collage of flowers and their animal helpers.

GLOSSARY

fruit (FROOT) the part of a plant that holds the seeds

nectar (NEK-ter) juice made by flowers for animals to drink

petals (PET-uhlz) parts of a flower that are usually brightly colored

pistils (PIS-tlz) parts of a flower inside of which seeds are made

pollen grains (POL-uhn GRAYNZ) dust-sized grains that make seeds in flowers

pollinated (POL-uh-ney-ted) having had pollen moved to one flower from another

stamens (STEY-mehnz) parts of a flower that make pollen

FIND OUT MORE

BOOKS

Aloian, Molly, and Bobbie Kalman. *The Life Cycle of a Flower*. New York: Crabtree Publishing Co., 2004.

Robbins, Ken. *Seeds*. New York: Atheneum Books for Young Readers, 2005.

WEB SITES

eNature—Field Guides: Wildflowers
www.enature.com/fieldguides/intermediate.asp?curGroupID=11
Learn about different kinds of wildflowers

Life Cycle of a Plant
www.bbc.co.uk/schools/ks2bitesize/science/activities/life_cycles.shtml
Practice naming flower parts

INDEX

ABOUT THE AUTHOR

Christine Petersen is a freelance writer and environmental educator who lives in Minnesota. When she is not writing, Christine enjoys kayaking, bird watching, and playing with her young son. She is the author of more than 20 books for young people.